From Disability To Self-Employment

… a journey for the few

Should you start or purchase a business?

Daniel Thomas McAneny

Daniel Thomas McAneny

6425 Grand Point Avenue

University Park FL 34201-2122

941-388-8975

ISBN: 0-9646490-2-0

Thanks to ...

... all the professionals in vocational rehabilitation and case management who have referred people to me over the years. They do the really hard work, making it possible for me to focus solely on helping motivated people make the best decisions.

Table of Contents

From the Author to the Reader

For the past 25 years I've been working with people on long term disability who wanted to either get a job or explore self-employment. In 1995 I wrote and published *So You're On Disability ... and you think you might want to get back into action.* It was a collection of half a dozen basic thoughts that my clients found helpful over the years, followed by stories about people on disability who had either landed jobs or started businesses.

This book includes a few of those basic thoughts in the first chapter, which address the emotional and psychological problems some people have when they go on disability. If you feel reasonably secure and confident in your new situation, you can skip the first chapter and go directly to the second.

While the first book was aimed primarily at people looking for a new job, this book is devoted exclusively to people who want to move from long term disability to self-employment. It takes you through the questions you need to ask yourself -- about you, the process, and the business – and it contains stories of people on disability who have started businesses.

Once you have the answers to the questions, there is no guarantee you will be successful. There never is in self-employment. But if you answer the questions, you will have a much better chance of success than if you forge ahead without those answers.

Please note, the answers may lead you to conclude that you shouldn't go into business for yourself, or at least not into the one you are planning. That's okay. Many people I've worked with are far better off for having turned in other directions. So please, read these pages with an open mind.

This book is not intended to help you analyze a large, complex business. Rather, it helps you undertake a simple, basic analysis of your chances for success in the particular small business of your choosing.

One of the main reasons many small businesses fail is that people do not sufficiently research their market ahead of time. They haven't thought through how they will attract customers or how they will get the sales they expect. In this book, you'll see a lot of emphasis on those topics.

It is **not** the purpose of this book to encourage you to go into business. Rather, the purpose is to help you evaluate whether the business you want to start or buy will be viable for you. Most people are **not** suited for self-employment.

If you haven't yet thought of a particular business, this book will provide direction on identifying one for which you might have a passion. But if you go through the process and still can't identify a business you feel enthusiastic about, it might be a sign that you aren't going to find one right for you. On the other hand, if you have the desire, you won't know that until you go through the process.

Chapter 1

Congratulations on Coming This Far!

If you're at the point where you're seriously considering self-employment, congratulations! From the day you first went out on disability, you've gone through a lot. Almost everyone on disability experiences initial feelings of isolation along with the frustration of inactivity.

Consider Bill.

For years, Bill was a high-powered financial wholesaler who sold financial products to other financial professionals. He had a heart attack in his late thirties which led him to diet religiously, exercise regularly, and give up drinking. When I met Bill in Boston he had been out for only a year and looked in perfect health. It was time for him to take the first steps toward getting back to work. But was he mentally ready?

> *"Dan, nobody knows what it means, what it does to your life. I've kept in close touch with my friends, lunch almost every week, and I've tried to explain it to them, but there are no words. The boredom and frustration are bad enough. But you also feel strange, as though what you used to do isn't real anymore. The world seems different, and you're not sure you fit in it the way you did before the disability."*

Or consider Fred. A brilliant manufacturing engineer, Fred relocated from California to Tennessee to lower his cost of living. For years, he made key contributions in the design and manufacture of products from tin cans to helicopters. After five years of being out, he was eager to return to work - and not just because he needed to earn more money.

> *"The financial problems are big, and I'm still dealing with back and leg pains. But what really gets me is that I don't have those interesting engineering*

projects anymore. It was a lot of fun figuring out
creative answers to tough design problems, and I
guess I was spoiled. It's not easy to fill your day when
you're used to doing what you love, and then you
can't do it anymore."

The story is the same even when the job isn't ideal. Here are the words of Marilyn, who held a job in electronics assembly before her back problems escalated.

"I never thought I had an especially good job, but
now I realize how much I miss seeing those people
every day, joking around, even working extra fast
when we had to. That job looks pretty good to me
now."

Phil, who worked in maintenance before his eye problems developed, felt the same way.

"Looking back, I see I enjoyed my job in ways I didn't
even know, but you could never have convinced me of
that back then."

No one but you can know what your disability means to you, not even another person with a long term disability. Life with a disability is just as individualized and isolated as the healthy life you had before. How can anyone else truly understand your particular blend of frustrations, anxieties, determination, hopes, fears, and all the subtle shades of emotions, or lack thereof, in between?

If you're on long term disability, it's likely that at one time, maybe not that long ago, you were working for an employer or were in your own business. You were healthy enough to do your job, and you identified with that job to some extent. You may have experienced some degree of discontent, or you may have loved every minute of it.

Regardless, your job gave you a place to go, as well as useful and productive things to do. At some level, it provided a comfortable feeling that, however important or unimportant you were in the overall scheme of things, you fit in. You were a functioning part of the world of commerce, a cog in the wheel of the great machine that makes the world hum. You were doing your part, however exalted or humble, in producing the goods and services that we all sell to one another to keep ourselves fed and clothed and housed.

You probably felt pretty good about it. At a minimum, it provided activity and filled your days with challenges, problems to solve, or interactions with others. You had talents and you used them to create, sell, operate, or analyze. You made things happen, helped others make things happen, or stopped things from happening. Your job gave you things to do that the rest of the world respected as honest labor, whatever its status.

But suddenly, one day, everyone else was going to work … and you weren't. Maybe it was because of an accident, an illness, a physical ailment that suddenly got worse, a stroke, or an operation. And it left you unable to perform as you always had -- and as you had always taken for granted.

That first day when you couldn't go to work like everyone else, the world shifted slightly. You perceived it from an angle you'd never experienced before. Things weren't the same and it felt uncomfortable. On the second day, your universe shifted a bit more.

Gradually, with each passing day, you began to inhabit a different psychological space. You didn't address the world the way you did for so long. Questions arose: Who am I if I'm no longer the person who does such-and-such each day? Am I still a valued and lovable person if I no longer achieve and produce? What is the significance of my life?

Concerns surface: Will I ever be productive again? Can I be happy doing something else – anything else? Am I falling behind? How will my family get by? Will I become a burden, or worse yet, a bore?

Depending on your answers to those kinds of questions, you gradually regained peace of mind and a healthy level of self-esteem.

Or things may have gone the other way...

By the time six months passed, you were in any number of emotional places. You may have fully expected to be "back in the swing of things" within a specified time period, and you kept yourself up-to-date in your chosen field.

Or, perhaps it was a little more complicated. Maybe you realized you couldn't go back to the same field any time soon... or ever. Maybe your employer didn't want you back or couldn't make room for you. Perhaps you could no longer run your business properly. A sense of isolation may have developed because you didn't know anyone else in the same difficult circumstances.

Financial problems may have developed, even with the cushion of benefit payments from your disability income policy. Marital and other relationships may have been tested, and the tests may have proved destructive. Friends may not have known how to respond so they slowly slipped away.

If there was physical pain, your whole world may have become focused on how to live with that pain. The energy and concentration it took to manage the pain became all-consuming, leaving little else of life to be experienced, and none of it savored. And if you needed medication to help cope, it may have robbed you of clear focus, energy, stamina, and zest for life.

Depending upon your circumstances, your reactions, and your individual makeup, a disability meant a temporary setback, or it brought your whole world crashing down, erasing all the familiar reference points by which you judged your daily experience, and distorting the standards and values you relied on to assign meaning to life.

Whatever meaning your disability had for you, you are indeed to be congratulated! If you are reading this, you're a survivor! You're already at Stage 2 or 3 of what Meredith Young-Sowers describes as the *three-stage healing framework:*

The Three-Stage Healing Framework

Even for people who are highly motivated to return to productive activity, one big obstacle is the feeling that the time since the onset of the disability is wasted time. It's seen as lost time that can never be regained.

If you look only at surface events, the time may indeed appear wasted, but if you look deeper, you'll find opportunity. I have seen this first-hand with many people. When I teach them how to apply the framework, it makes a lot of sense to them. It shifts their focus away from the frustration of "wasted time" and onto the anticipation of exploring new opportunities.

Within the Healing Framework, the time from *disability onset* to *productivity and personal fulfillment* is seen as a healing process with three stages. The first stage is not one where you immediately go out and start knocking on the world's door, but more of an internal experience.

Stage 1... Making The Internal Adjustments

Most people start at Stage 1, an internal process. There is a lot of work done in this stage, as people gradually get adjusted to a brand new set of circumstances. They try to regain equilibrium while new roles, rules, and limitations are thrust upon them.

This is hard work, and those who come through it without being defeated, with a determination to get back to meaningful daily activity, can be very proud of this achievement. It's the phase where the challenge is the greatest, where the most work is done, and the most progress made. Those who come through it intact are survivors. The fact that the work is primarily internal, rather than external, does not detract from its significance.

As soon as people realize that their time has not been wasted and that significant internal adjustments have been made, they understand that they knew this all along. It just took someone else to acknowledge what they already knew internally.

11

When they do acknowledge it, they are immediately freed from the energy-consuming focus on having "wasted all this time." They understand instead that they have successfully met one of life's toughest challenges. It's as though a little explosion goes off, and they are now filled with excitement, anticipation, and a new surge of energy.

As one person put it, he was suddenly "galvanized into action." A great burden was lifted from his shoulders as he realized that getting rid of the burden was as simple as putting it down.

The realization dawns, "Hey, I haven't been wasting time. I've been doing great things. Let's get on with it!"

This stage can take weeks, months or even years. There are no rules about the right amount of time, but people know when it happens. They think about how they're going to get back into action, and what they might do that will be appealing and rewarding, even if getting back into action means less security than regular disability payments. Their need to live a productive life outweighs those concerns. They're willing to take the risk. Fortunately, most disability policies have provisions that can help minimize that risk, and make it a carefully calculated one.

Stage 2 ..... Finding Something To Get Excited About

I usually enter people's lives towards the end of the first stage. My "clients," as I call them even though the insurance companies pay me, are ready for the second stage, which is *finding something to get excited about.*

When they find a direction they can get excited about, it unleashes a fountain of positive energies. Now they can focus on actions toward attaining a worthwhile goal. No longer do they see their actions as haphazard; instead, they feel a steady surge of well-directed energy, like a laser beam going after a specific target with a tremendous amount of concentrated power.

For people who've been on disability for a while, it can be a tough challenge to find something to get excited about. If you've already found a business that excites you, good for you. If you're searching for one, we'll touch shortly on the *Close Encounter* approach that's helpful for moving through this stage.

Stage 3 ..... Opening Up To the World In A Mutual Give-and-Take

The third stage in the healing framework is *opening up to the world in a mutual give-and-take effort* aimed at reaching the goal. Those on disability continue to *give* to others whenever possible, but also must learn to *receive* graciously, letting others help in the effort and enjoy the good feelings that come from being a giver. This mutual interchange of positive energies in the give-and-take is what completes the healing, both on the spiritual and physical levels.

It is not reaching the goal itself, but the process of getting there, that completes the healing. About 90% of my clients turn out to be givers who haven't yet learned to be gracious receivers. When they realize how much others gain as givers, they understand they've been cutting off half the natural energy flow between humans. They gain greater appreciation for the healing effects of a two-way flow of that energy.

The timing is quite fortunate for learning that lesson. Whenever you are attempting to start a business, you can use all the help that might come your way. Developing a business plan involves a lot of interaction with others in a purposeful, systematic way, and that give-and-take provides a needed feeling of momentum.

The *Close Encounter* Approach

In discussing the three-stage healing process, the point was made that, for many people on disability, the second stage -- finding something to get excited about -- can be difficult. People on long term disability tend to beat themselves up if they aren't able to generate enthusiasm for a new goal, but most need to find a new field in which they have little experience and it's unrealistic to expect to get excited about something new and distant.

Do you know anyone who can get truly excited about something

13

they've never gotten close to? The answer here is to release yourself from the unrealistic expectation that you can get excited about something from a distance.

That's where I come in. I help identify goals that clients *might get excited about if they got close to them.* Then I provide whatever they need to get closer to those goals. In the process they find out for themselves whether they still want those goals when they are up close. I call it *Close Encounter With Stated Goals.*

Very important here is the perspective, which says that if you get close to a goal and find you don't like it, that's real progress!!

Why? Because we've eliminated a "phantom goal," which allows you to focus your energies more clearly on another goal. In the meantime, you develop a better understanding of what you really want, based on real-life experiences, not just on guesses made at a distance.

Once you understand that it's okay to go after something, find you don't like it, drop it, and pursue something else, you'll lose a lot of your anxiety and will make real progress. It isn't even something you have to think about. Your *feelings* reveal soon enough whether a particular option is right for you. The whole process flows smoothly and naturally.

The *Close Encounter* approach enables you to seek out and discard a number of options, if necessary, without feeling guilty or pressured about it. And the funny thing is, with all that freedom to pursue endlessly, few people go through more than three or four options without finding the one that they *know* is right for them. Sometimes it takes a while, and sometimes the process is completed quickly.

You may be concerned that if you try this approach in attempting to identify a business to get excited about, you may have endless *close encounters.* My advice? Press on anyway. It may simply mean you have some fears you haven't yet recognized, and at some point you'll need to face them. Maybe you aren't as motivated to start or buy a business as you thought, which is helpful to discover. Or maybe you haven't yet found the business that's right for you. The only way to find which of these is true in your case is to keep on moving ahead.

Burt is a good example. He had worked on ships in the underwater oil fields in the Gulf of Mexico and other places, maintaining and repairing large engines. It was demanding work and he enjoyed it.

By the time he'd been out for a couple of years with knee and ankle problems, he told me he couldn't take the slow pace any longer and needed to find a suitable business that would make enough money and keep him occupied every day.

We started out looking at trailer camps and motorcycle repair, then at a small trucking company, and some repair businesses that would put his mechanical knowledge to good use, so long as other people could handle the physical functions he could no longer perform.

Even though he worked diligently to identify something suitable, it took him the better part of a year -- much longer than usual -- but he eventually found the perfect business for him… operating a *Rover* sailboat, often referred to as a "pirate boat" along the lines of an 1800s schooner, and using it as both a charter sailboat and for training young people to sail in southern Florida.

Action ..... The Antidote to Isolation and the Key to the "Opportunity Collision"

Doing the research for a business plan, or for finding a business you like, requires a lot of action. There are many wonderful things about taking action. The best is, *action displaces fear!*

World War II hero, Audie Murphy, was asked if he was afraid when he charged enemy trenches with a grenade in his hand. His answer is worth remembering.

He was actually shaking with fear, he said, up to the moment when he pulled the pin on the grenade and started running toward the enemy. At that moment, he explained, as soon as he got into action, there just wasn't any room for fear. He didn't have to think about or fight the fear. Quite simply, he was preoccupied with taking action, and there was no room in his mind, no time, and no place inside him left over for fear. In his opinion, you can't be acting and fearing at the same time, even if you want to.

Action *displaces* fear, he said. Just as when you put a ship in water, it displaces the water. The ship and the water can't be in the same place at the same time, and so it is with action and fear.

If you substitute *anxiety or doubt* for the word *fear,* the same principle applies. If any of those feelings have crowded your mind or clouded your spirits, know that part of the answer to achieving peace of mind and a sense of progress is to get into action.

Another positive is that acting *gets you past indecision.* There's a reason you often hear people faced with a problem say, "Let's get past this thing," or "Let's get this behind us." The one sure way to stop worrying about whether you are going to make the right decision, and to get a problem or challenge behind you, is to *act* on it.

Still another positive… action *feels good!* Think about any time when you were taking action on something you cared about or enjoyed. Maybe it was helping someone else, building something, planting a shrub or garden, learning to ride a bike, or making a big contribution on the job. Can you remember how it felt at those moments when you were taking those actions? Maybe you'd thought about doing them for some time without much feeling. But when you started acting, *it felt good,* didn't it?

Getting into action can be especially significant for those with disabilities. Most of them miss the interaction they used to have with people during the course of their work day. Almost by definition, *action means interacting with other people*, and as that happens, bit by bit, you feel more connected to others.

Action also *creates its own energy force*, and you can feel yourself uniting with others in spirit. The combined energies of your action and theirs become almost palpable. The math always works out so that 1+1 equals more than 2 -- in some cases, substantially more.

If you want to get a business started, the single most important thing about action is that it is *The Key to the Opportunity Collision.* There's a world out there where a lot of things are happening, a lot of businesses are growing, and thousands of people are realizing they need to buy a product or service like yours... but none of that has a chance of touching your life if you're not out there *acting.*

If the following is not one of the universal laws of nature, then it should be classified as a most-of-the-time law of nature: people who are actively seeking a specific type of opportunity will, in the course of their efforts, be presented with *at least one opportunity they never expected and weren't looking for.* I've based this "law" on the experiences of hundreds of clients, and I've long since stopped being surprised when it happens.

Plans for a business can take unexpected turns. The world becomes a more exciting place when you're out there in action. Who wants to know exactly how their life will play out for years ahead? That's boring. Secure maybe, but still boring.

When you're out there in the path of opportunity, any day, at any moment, in almost any place, an unexpected opportunity can come out of nowhere and sideswipe you when you're not looking. How exciting! All you need to do is stay in action and keep your mind open to the good things happening to you and for you. You may find new ways to approach the business you're planning, or find an entirely new business to develop.

Chapter 2

Start By Answering Questions About Yourself

If you are thinking about starting, buying, or buying into a business, it is helpful to ask yourself questions about three subjects -- yourself, the process you'll need to go through, and the business. Consider these questions about yourself:

Am I Cut Out to Run a Business?

Only a small percentage of people are cut out for running a business, but that includes more people, and more personality types, than you might think. **It is not the purpose of this book to encourage you to start a business,** but to help protect you from starting one that has little chance of meeting your income goals.

Still, many people rule themselves out before they've even taken the time to consider all the factors. They think, "I'm afraid to take a risk," but forget that there are *degrees* of risk. Risks can often be minimized to the point where someone averse to a big risk might feel comfortable taking the smaller risk. For some, the risk of remaining on disability is perceived to be greater than the risk of starting or buying a business.

Will Self-Employment Appeal to Me?

A number of people on disability fall into a category that makes self-employment appealing to them. It's possible you might fit into one or more of these categories:

- **Unreliable as an employee in a traditional work setting.**

    Some people know their disability will cause them to miss days, or to take long or frequent breaks, so they can't honestly tell an employer they'd be reliable for the standard workday on a consistent basis. In their own business, however, they can work their schedules around their needs.

- **Can't live on benefit income**

  Many people have told me that with disability as their only source of income, their financial situation worsened each month as expenses exceeded income. Long term disability benefits are usually 60% of base income, so a 40% cut is tough enough, but many people also relied on income above their base, making the cut significantly greater. For example, a woman in California who used to sell cosmetics started a home-based dermassage business because a large part of her income had been commissions. She couldn't get by on 60% of her base.

- **Benefits end at 65.**

  A 58-year-old mechanical contractor in Baltimore who'd had a heart attack knew he'd be in financial trouble after 65 if something didn't change. He bought part interest in a contracting company, which not only increased his income dramatically, but also, as part owner, he could work as long as he wished. He planned to keep going past 70. He could also work limited hours and take a nap if he needed it.

- **No job security.**

  Dozens of people over the years have voiced their fear of getting a new job, thereby losing their disability benefit, then losing the new job. They fear ending up with no job and no benefits. As owners of a business, they know there's always a risk the business might fail, but on the upside, they can't be fired, and they'd rather have their future in their own hands.

- **View self-employment as a path to increasing income and building equity.**

  A lot of people see operating a business as an opportunity to increase income over past levels and build equity. Many clients who held mechanically oriented jobs have started service businesses. Others might buy convenience stores. In most cases, projected income is significantly more than they made as employees. They also believe they can build the business so it will be worth something, and they can sell it in the future or pass it on to their children.

- **A path to traditional employment.**

   One client who started a filtration consulting business knew that as he built a customer base, he would likely be recruited by a larger filter distribution company, which would please him. Another client who started a catering business was offered a manager's job by a fast food chain. A small percentage of clients like these see self-employment as a means to make themselves more attractive as employees.

For people on disability who…

   - need to earn more money

   - can't stand inactivity

   - don't believe they could be reliable employees

   - might need to lie down at times during the day

   - fear getting a job and then losing it along with benefits

…some form of self-employment can be an appealing option, and may be the most realistic choice.

How much do I really know about the proposed business?

   Many people who never before considered running their own business find that they are indeed suited to it. They have carefully researched and planned their business. They're realistic about their chances for success, not just blindly hopeful.

   If you haven't yet researched a business in depth, it isn't logical to think you could develop confidence about it. That lack of confidence in the early stages is not necessarily a sign that you aren't meant to run a business. It's a sign that you need to learn more. In the process, you'll either develop the confidence or not, and you can act accordingly. We'll explore this area further in Chapter 3.

What are my strengths? What functions can I fill in the business? Can I get someone else to handle the functions where I'm not strong?

A man who wanted to run a ferry service in Alaska was not sales-oriented. He found that he didn't need to be a salesman to be successful. There was so much demand that all he needed to do was keep his boat running smoothly, remain friendly, and be punctual - three things he'd been doing well for a long time.

In another instance, a financial manager without sales experience found he could sign up the owners of convenience stores for his specialized vending business simply by taking them through some brief financial calculations.

In still another instance, an ex-Air Force Captain with a back problem couldn't do anything too physically demanding but he was skilled in sales. He joined with an experienced window washer to create a successful business of cleaning multi-story commercial buildings in Honolulu. Each man filled the functions in which they felt comfortable.

Am I being honest with myself?

Making a sound decision about a business involves a careful analysis of yourself, your strengths, and preferences. People have different needs. Some prefer the social aspects of working with others. Others know they won't handle the stress well, or they don't have the self-discipline required.

Some find they have strengths and skills they didn't know they had, and the idea of having their own business or consultancy just feels right. Others might determine that they don't have what it takes to make the business successful. That may be an indication the business is not for them, but it may also be a sign that they need to think in terms of joining with someone else.

Regardless of the outcome, you owe it to yourself to address all these questions, and to be honest with yourself. This requires a careful examination of what you truly believe about yourself, being as objective as you possibly can.

What Do You Believe About Yourself?

It's always to your advantage if you can choose among many realistic options. Your beliefs about yourself can narrow or broaden those options. The number of viable options open to you will often vary in direct proportion to your beliefs about ...

- **The functions you can fill**

    If you are not joining with someone else and believe you're not a very good salesperson, limit your business choices to those which do not depend on strong selling skills. Likewise, if you can sell but you're not very good at managing operations, then stay away from businesses where efficient operations are the key to success. But before you cut yourself out of an option, *examine carefully why you believe you're not good at something*. Sometimes we mistakenly develop limiting beliefs early in life and never give ourselves a chance to use the talents we actually possess.

- **Your personal strengths**

    You might have limiting beliefs about your personal strengths. A business might require that you relate well to all types of people, and you might believe you're not very strong there. Again, ask yourself if that is because you tried and failed to relate to many types of people, or simply because you never had the opportunity?

    Too often we believe that because we haven't yet tried something, we aren't very good at it. One client who thought he couldn't deal effectively with a lot of people at trade shows, where he would need to sell his hand-carved pipes, found to his delight that he was a natural at building rapport with anyone who stopped by his booth.

- **The value you can deliver**

    Sometimes people don't appreciate the value they can deliver. A kitchen contractor in New England felt he could no longer deliver value to customers when his legs no longer allowed him to stand on ladders for long periods. A careful examination of his beliefs made him realize that the value he delivered depended primarily on his ability to design and implement precision carpentry. By finding a helper who could stand on ladders for long periods, and who could also work to his demanding standards, he was soon delivering exceptional value to customers again.

Whatever beliefs you hold about what you can and cannot do, it pays to regularly examine them. Figure out why you believe you can't fill a particular function, or that you don't possess a particular strength. *If you'd like to develop more positive beliefs about yourself, try using Selective Perception:*

Go back through your past, concentrating only on those times where people said positive things about you, or reacted favorably to you.

Write down every positive instance you can remember, and keep adding to the list whenever you can. Ignore any and all negatives, as if they never existed. Take out your list a few times a week and reflect on all those positive events and statements.

Before you know it, you'll find that concentrating on all those positives has left no room for negative or limiting beliefs about yourself, and you'll feel confident that you can accomplish a number of things you've never done before.

Chapter 3

Questions About the Process

In chapter 2, we explored questions about you. Now it is time to look at questions about the process. You'll need the answers to these questions as you explore self-employment:

What should I expect emotionally as I explore the feasibility of a business?

You need to be prepared for an emotional rollercoaster. It doesn't always happen, but if and when it does, it is important for you to be aware that major ups and downs are a common occurrence when starting a business. When you explore a new business, there is a great degree of enthusiasm. As you learn more about the challenges involved, fear and doubt arise as you realize all that you don't know.

This stage is actually good, because it stimulates you to learn more. As you do, you once again regain a feeling of confidence and enthusiasm ... until the increased knowledge leads to an awareness of many other things you don't know, leading to doubt and fear again. That's followed by still more learning, leading to more confidence, and the cycle goes on.

The rollercoaster leads to one of two conclusions. Either you give up at a point in the cycle where fear and doubt are greatest, or you forge ahead and establish the business when enthusiasm and confidence are at their highest point.

Either outcome is okay, and is probably the right outcome for each individual.

How can I identify businesses suitable for me to explore?

As you think about options, if you don't have a strong interest in any particular business, here are a few considerations that can lead to identification of new business options suitable for you:

- Take time to reflect on all your interests. Make a list of them and discuss them with family and friends to determine any and all businesses the list might suggest.

- Make a list of all the people you know who are in businesses, and reflect on whether one or more of those businesses might appeal to you.

- Think about any business where you might have thought, "I'd like to be in that business."

- Think about any recurring impulses you've had to explore a particular business or learn more about it.

- Think of any business where someone might have remarked to you that you'd be very good in it.

- Contact business brokers, locally or on the internet, following the advice in this book. Keep notes on every business you learn about from them, especially as to what you like and dislike about the business.

- Meet with friends, one-on-one or in a group, and ask them to brainstorm with you concerning businesses they think you might do well to explore.

- If you know any business consultants, lawyers, bankers or accountants, meet with them for the same purpose.

What if I make the wrong decision?

There is no right or wrong here. What each person does is probably the right path for that individual at that time. The important thing is to learn as much as possible before making the decision. Then, whether it's a go or no-go, it's the right decision for you.

Knowing about the emotional rollercoaster ahead of time might give you the determination to persevere and keep on exploring when you've reached your first or second fear/doubt crest. That way, when you make the decision to start a business or not, you'll be making it with a stronger base of experience and knowledge. That increases the chances it's the right decision.

What happens after I realize a business is not right for me?

There have been instances where people researched a business for quite some time, then decided it was not suitable or viable for them. In many cases, it wasn't too long before they found an alternate business and went ahead with it.

Here are two typical examples. A woman in Colorado with an illness that limited her energy was forced to give up on a cookie baking company in which she'd made a lot of progress. It wasn't more than six months later when she and her husband settled on operating resort cabins, which they did successfully. Her function was to handle the front desk, and she had plenty of energy for that.

A man in Indiana intent on a used auto sales business finally realized he couldn't do it. Three months later, he was in the business of rental income property. In nine months, he was doing quite well.

Very often, when people expend a lot of energy on exploring a business, and they get thwarted for one reason or another, it seems that energy has built to a point where it must find some expression. Apparently, if it is denied in one business, it will find an outlet in another. For that reason, it should not be a cause for concern if you spend a lot of time and energy on a business only to conclude that it is not suitable for you. Something good will eventually come of all your effort – either another business or a decision not to start a business at all.

Is there a practical, helpful approach I can use for exploring businesses?

Yes there is. As mentioned above, you needn't worry about wasting your time -- or chalking up a failure -- when you explore a business. There is no wasted time. You learn by the experience. And you are better off for it.

Simply use the *Close Encounter* approach described earlier. It has worked well for many people attempting to find a suitable business. If you choose to explore a business, spend a lot of time "getting closer to it," and if you find it is not for you, you have not failed and should not be disappointed. Instead, consider that:

First, you have cleared away an option that wasn't right for you, and you can't go after a more suitable business until you get the first one out of the way.

Second, you've gained momentum in the process -- that energy mentioned earlier. Whenever you get into action exploring something, it begins to build energy and momentum.

Third, you've established some criteria for what you like and don't like, which will guide your next selection of a business to explore, bringing you closer to the option best suited for you.

Using this approach removes pressure. You realize you don't need to find absolutely the right business before you investigate it. You can explore any business, devote time to it, and know that the time is not wasted, even if you eventually reject it.

Be assured, once you get started, your path will eventually take you to the options that make most sense for you. Does that guarantee you will be successful? No, but it will substantially increase the odds in your favor. So if you relax and use the *Close Encounter* approach, chances are you'll wind up in a pretty good place -- emotionally, and in terms of the business you choose.

If you want to go into business, but don't yet have a firm idea about what you'd like, the following list of some businesses I've helped others explore might stimulate your thinking.

Startups

Cowboy hat manufacturer/retailer in TX
Primary care practice in HI
Commercial plumbing in CA
Used car dealership in CA
Cajun restaurant in Upstate NY
Barbecue stand in US Virgin Islands
Taxidermy – several states
MLM discount travel in NM
Personal historian/videographer New England
Software for applications development in NM
Legal healthcare practice in Sacramento, CA
Executive protection services in Washington, D.C.
Dog training and care in TX
Upscale portrait photography in SC & TN
Commercial photography in CO
Men's vests manufacturer in Peru
Wellness Center in WY
Handyman / Repair business in several states
Laughter session business in PA
Mechanical repair & office rental in ND
Specialty chemicals sales rep in WI
Equipment leasing in TX
Accounting and bookkeeping in FL
Concrete resurfacing in WY
Rental income property in several locations
Egg farmer (small scale) in Maine
Cannabinologist medical practice in CA
Labor relations consultancy/ training in CA
Specialized trucking in IN
Workers Comp insurance agency in NC & FL
Jewelry making in several states
Engine repair in OK
Costumier business in Nevada
Propane safety consulting in CO
Heating, ventilating, A/C in several states
Home repair and remodeling
Computer-aided (CAD) drawings for homes
Gym

Curves franchise
Electronic medical claims billing
Motorcycle repair
Lunch truck
Wooden products (several)
Event-based/celebrity marketing/promotion
Non-profit health screening
Medical practice management consultant
Spiritual realization via aesthetic reification
Theater-based learning in public schools
Home builder
Industrial filter sales
Cement contractor
Used cars (three)
Self-storage units
Ferry service in Alaska
Mobile home broker in GA
Silk screen printing
Pipe carving
Thermal Imaging
Convenience store (several)
Beauty salon / Skin treatment (several)
Printing/plate making
Landscape equipment sales / repair
Tutoring
Outdoor shooting range
Private investigation firm
Gun repair
Catering (several)
Flower shop (several)
Candy / fudge making
Bowling tournament promotion
Phone card distributing
Toy Shop
Specialized travel agency (two)
Bridal / floral shop
Electrical /electronic auto repair
Tree trimming (two)
Skyscraper window washing

Elevator advertising
Growing flowers
Resort cabins
Specialty cookies
Mechanical contractor
Photography – consumer (several)
Arts and crafts store
Ceramics store and teaching
Fine furniture crafting
Tractor-based services
Septic tank installation / road building - MN
Secretarial services
Mortgage banking brokerage
Fishing guide
Website design
Computer / software consultancy (several)
Crane safety training
Go-cart sales, service, accessories
Specialized welding / crane fabrication
Raising Alpaca
Costume manufacture and rental
Family historian
Massage / Paraffin/Personal Trainer / Gym
Dog Grooming
Wine Distributor
Telecom Master Agent
Barge Boat Operation
RV Park
Travel Agency – Ocean Cruises
Cleaning services
Events promotion
Music arrangements & sequencing
Therapeutic massage
Writing services
Bakery/deli
Teen activities center
Claims Adjusting in WA
Children's parties & fitness
Trucking – long distance

Trucking -- local aggregate hauling
Conveyor system installation
Embroidery
Sales rep for imported furniture
Locator for real estate auctions
Stable & feed store in WV
9-hole golf course
Legal practice
Computer repair & user training
Clock repair in OH
Automation consulting in CO
Golf club repair
Conference / event admin services

Improving or Evaluating a Business
Beeswax candles
Blueberry farming
Christmas store
Adhesives formulator
Brake lining supplier
Locksmith
Painting contractor
Hydraulic cylinder replacement
Industrial filter design/fabrication and sales
Several consultancies
Employee leasing organization
Boat repair
Independent counselor (several)
Soap making
Specialized boat manufacturing
Architectural firm
Sign fabrication
Unclaimed property retrieval
Restaurants
Restaurant furniture refurbishing
Auto restoration
Veterinary practice – cats only
Medical practices
Manufacturer of dog training collars

Chapter 4

Questions About the Business

There are eight basic questions you can ask when attempting to evaluate whether a business is feasible for you. They are:

1. What is the nature of the business?

2. Is there really a market out there?

3. How big is the market?

4. Why do I expect to get enough sales to make the business feasible?

5. Will profit margins and costs give me the income I'm targeting?

6. What will my startup costs be? And how much cash do I need?

7. Have I considered the risks and tried to minimize them?

8. Why am I qualified to run the business?

If you know the answers, you've got a plan.

Whether you realize it or not, when you've got the answers to those questions, you've got a business plan. Many people who have started businesses say that if they had foreseen at the outset all the problems they would encounter, they would never have started the business in the first place. Yet, looking back, they are glad they did.

You might ask yourself, why bother with a plan at all? In fact, unless your business is complex or will require a number of investors, it's probably wise to stay away from a complicated business plan.

On the other hand, there are a few solid reasons why you ought to have a *simple* plan. First, you'll have something by which to measure your progress. If you're not doing as well as you expected, you can look at your plan to see why you're not doing what you expected. The plan will make it easier to change things if necessary, or do more of the right things.

Second, it helps to know how long you'll be putting money into the business before you start taking it out. If your plan can tell you that ahead of time, you won't have any surprises. Surprises can be very painful in the area of cash flow.

Third, a plan forces you to start envisioning step-by-step how your business will proceed, so it begins to take on an emotional reality for you, and your feelings can tell you ahead of time whether a business is really for you.

Fourth, it can help reveal any flaws in the way you propose to do business, and perhaps uncover a risk or two you hadn't thought of. Risks and flaws that are identified early can be corrected early, before much damage is done, improving your chances for success.

Let's review each of the 8 basic questions at the beginning of the chapter:

1. What Is the Nature of the Business?

You might think this is obvious, and doesn't require much thought, but it is surprising how often people haven't thought this through carefully. Sometimes the proposed business is a combination of two or three different businesses, and people don't know what percentage of the total each business will be.

For example, a man intending to publish family reunion yearbooks also wanted to start a printing business and a pennysaver publication for which he would solicit advertising. The three businesses are quite distinct, and in his case, it helped to figure out which of the three would be the primary business, when each could realistically be started, and when each might become profitable.

33

In another case, a person wanted to go into the business of making and repairing golf clubs, but hadn't given much thought to what percentage of the business would be in repair work. This was an important area to address because the profit ratios for building clubs versus repairing clubs are quite different.

If your business can be explained simply in a sentence or two, write it down. On reflection, if you realize it involves more than one kind of activity, be sure you include them all. Also try to estimate what percentage of the total a particular segment of the business will be. This simple step can be very revealing in telling you what your business is actually about.

2. Is There Really a Market Out There?

Sometimes the answer is obviously yes, especially if you are buying an existing business, or if others are already prospering in it. But you may want to start a business where you're not sure about the demand. The easiest and fastest way to gauge demand is to go directly to the people you would expect to be customers, and talk with them.

A man who wanted to build bamboo fishing poles made one quick call to the publisher of a catalog that carried fishing poles. (Today he'd also contact sites online that sell them.) He found that there was a market for what he intended to make, and that when such poles were included in catalogs, they sold out in a matter of weeks.

On the other hand, a woman who wanted to go into the decorative basket business found that, for the types of baskets she wanted to produce at a certain price level, there simply wasn't a market. Firsthand research of that nature can give you immediate answers as to whether or not you really have a market out there.

3. How Big Is the Market?

It helps to know how big the market is, because then it's easier to figure out what share of the market you need to capture in order to reach your goals. A man in the Pittsburgh area researched the tree removal and trimming business and found that all six people in his area had 10 to 16-week backlogs.

Another man investigating the same business in the Philadelphia area found that two large companies dominated the business in his region, that smaller operators didn't have enough business, and that a number of them had given up on the business in the last few years. In both cases, the market itself was plenty big, but getting into that market was another question.

If you have no idea of the size of your market, there are a number of things you can do. A lot of information is available on the Internet. Use the advanced search feature of search engines and put in the exact phrase that applies to your market, as well as other words you do or don't want. It tends to lower the number of sites you need to search before getting to those that are most helpful

You can visit the business reference section of a local library, and speak with the reference librarian. Often you can look up statistics on Standard Metropolitan Statistical Areas to find important characteristics about the population you intend to serve, such as income and age. Trade publications for the industry you are exploring can also be helpful, giving you information about industry size and how it breaks down by major sectors.

It's a good idea to contact an industry association. You can find almost any association in *Encyclopedia of Associations*. There is a helpful keyword index that contains information about the association, as well as contact information for key people. Associations often have information such as how much population is required to support a particular business.

You can also use a Dun & Bradstreet or other directory of corporations. Such directories allow you to tally up the revenues of existing businesses in your area. Or, if you can get a reasonable estimate of the size of one business in your area, perhaps from an accountant or banker, you can roughly calculate the total of all such businesses. Franchise information can also be very informative. *Entrepreneur* Magazine can give you a quick overall idea of franchise costs and terms in a variety of business categories, and you can proceed to explore further from there.

As mentioned earlier, one of the best ways to estimate potential revenues is to visit with prospective customers. If they can give you a good idea of whether they'd purchase from you, and if so how much, it will help you calculate a realistic estimate of your potential market.

Calling on people in a similar business, but in another region of the country, can be helpful. If people don't fear you'll become a competitor, they can be forthcoming with valuable information about how they got started, how they did in the first year, what unexpected problems they encountered, etc.

4. Why Do I Expect to Get Enough Sales to Make the Business Feasible?

This is the most important question to answer. Unless you can get enough information to answer this question with some degree of confidence, your degree of risk will likely be high. So let's take a look at what steps you can take.

It's helpful to ask why customers will buy. It may be location or habit or convenience. In some instances, you might be relying on your past sales achievements, especially if the type of sale in the new business will be similar. At other times you may be filling a demand that is so great, sales are almost a given, which was the case for one fellow starting an auto repair business where existing shops had long waiting times. People may buy for price or because what you offer will help them earn more money. Whatever the reason for customer purchases, you should be able to identify it.

When addressing this question, you should give consideration to just how intense the competition is. A West Coast woman intending to enter the fish wholesaling business determined that the market for some of the largest restaurants in the area was very intense, but that small and mid-sized restaurants promised relatively easy entry into the market. In five conversations, she obtained four tentative commitments from restaurant owners to buy at least some of their seafood from her, if she were to go into business.

When considering whether you can get enough sales, you should also consider whether special sales, marketing and promotion skills are necessary to be successful in the business. If you don't have them, then logically you'd want to be able to hire someone who does. Then, in your plan you need to take into account the cost of that person's salary, commissions and benefits.

Ask yourself if you are selling something people already use, or will you have to convince people to start using your product or service? If you are trying to introduce a new concept, it may take a long time before people accept it to the degree that you can build significant sales. You need to know how you will support yourself during the "missionary stage," when you are introducing the concept.

As for your personal success in sales, your past experience or current activity can be a good indicator that you will be able to generate sufficient sales to make a business feasible. Just be sure the type of selling in which you excel is the type that's required to make your intended business successful. Selling shoes at retail is quite different from selling catering services, and both are quite different from selling packaging machinery. Take into account any special advantage you have that will give you an edge. It could be your knowledge, contacts, or past experience in the field

Overall, answering Question #4 is the key to success for most new or small businesses. Statistics over the years continually show that a major cause for the failure of new businesses is a failure to generate sufficient sales. Looking closely at this question upfront may lead you to adopt a different strategy and become more successful right from the start.

Again, for most small businesses, the single most important question to ask is this: **Why am I assuming that, on a daily basis, I'll be able to get the number of customers and sales I need to make this business successful?**

It's easy enough to figure out expenses and startup costs, but the tough part is answering that question. It is worth spending whatever time is required to get answers which reassure you that your estimates of how much business you can generate are reasonable.

A fellow starting a welding business in New York State thought he could get enough business to get by. It wasn't until he went out and talked with a dozen prospective customers that he received reassurances he could get even more business than he had counted on.

Another man in Vermont assumed he could sell a certain number of parts and decals for go-karts for his proposed business. Firsthand discussions with prospects showed he could not only sell specific quantities, but that he could expect steady revenue from a related dynamometer service, which made the business much more feasible.

A woman in New Mexico wanted to open a toy store in a particular town, but didn't know if she could sell x number of toys per day at an average price of y. We knew what x and y had to be for the business to make enough income because we knew what her costs and profit margins would be. But why should we assume she could sell even a single toy per day?

She didn't know, until she got the input we requested from her own extensive research over two months -- on the Internet, with owners of shops in similar towns, industry association officials, consultants, magazine editors and several local focus groups composed of wives and mothers from area families.

A woman in Minnesota wanted to open a coffee and sandwich shop, but couldn't give a single good reason why she expected to sell the number of pieces of pie, cups of coffee, and sandwiches each day that she'd need to generate the income she required. Talks over two months with owners of similar shops, traffic counts, discussions with suppliers, and her own observations of the number of items sold in similar shops, eventually gave her the answers we needed for a plan.

A man operating a septic tank installation business couldn't answer why he thought he could do enough installations to grow his business and earn enough income. We gathered statistics from the County on new home building, information on new requirements for upgrading existing tanks, and performed an analysis of the competition and how long it took them to build their businesses. We made a decision that he should put more emphasis on the site clearing, road building and hauling parts of his business. All of this information helped put a realistic plan together with financial projections that would likely prove accurate.

In each of these examples and dozens more, people had no idea whether they'd be successful, why, or how successful they could be, until they addressed Question #4 and took whatever time and effort required to get meaningful answers.

5. Will Profit Margins and Costs Give Me the Income I'm Targeting?

When you talk about gross profit margins, you are usually talking about selling products at retail. The gross profit is the selling price for the product, less the cost of it. So if you sell a clock for $100, and it cost you $60, then your gross profit is $40. Your gross profit margin is 40% of sales in that example, and your markup percentage is $40 divided by $60, or 66.6%.

In any business that sells products, you need to know if your gross profits are going to be high enough to cover all your other expenses other than just the product itself, such as rent, advertising, sales and administrative expenses. Some retail businesses fail because their markups are not high enough and their gross profit is too low to cover those costs.

The answer to Question #5 requires that you anticipate all expenses fairly accurately. Envisioning how you will operate, week by week and month by month, put down figures for expected income and expenses each month.

For expenses, start by listing the types of expenses you know you will incur. Then, estimate remaining expenses. Sometimes, the best you can do is to make best guesses. In that case, make two sets of guesses -- one conservative and the other optimistic.

When you make an estimate, **make a note of the assumption underlying that estimate.** In other words, if you estimate printing costs of $200 per month, make a note on what you assumed in order to reach that figure. You may have assumed that you would order the printing of 500 flyers per month, and 300 reprints of an article. By keeping track of your assumptions, you will know how it will affect operations if you need to change your figures later.

It is important not to overlook expense categories or overestimate profit margins when putting together financial projections. Several people planning to open retail stores have simply assumed they could sell a certain amount each month at 50% gross profit (100% markup). They later learned that because of price competition or buyer resistance, they could only average 30% gross profit.

Let's take a quick look at how disastrous that can be for the survival of the business. If they expected to sell $30,000 per month of products at 50% gross margin, they'd have $15,000 per month gross profit to cover expenses. If they planned on $10,000 per month expenses, that would still leave $5000 per month profit.

Now consider what happens if they find they can sell at only a 30% profit margin. Gross profit every month drops to $9000. With expenses at $10,000, they are now losing $1000 per month. If they cannot quickly cut expenses, increase sales, or increase profit margins, they need to get out of the business.

When you are thinking about income and expenses, make sure you are not missing any of the following, if they apply to your business:

Sales (Unit Sales)
Lease Income

Bad Checks
Credit card charges
Credit card reversals
Refunds

Commissions
Local / State taxes
Staff Salaries
Casual Labor
Benefits / Payroll
Outside Contractors

Cost of Goods Sold
Raw Materials
Overhead
Transportation & Storage

Rent & Utilities
Depreciation
Lease Costs
Interest

Travel & Entertainment
Internet / Website
Advertising & Promotion
Sales Costs
Printing
Postage
Office Supplies

Insurance / Legal fees
Accounting
Licenses
Memberships

Subscriptions
Training
Software

6. What Will Your Startup Costs Be? And How Much Cash Do You Need?

In order to answer Question #5, you needed to make your best guess about cash inflow and outflow every month for at least the first year, if not three years. If the business is not going to generate income right away, you'll have an idea of how much money you expect to lose each month before you start making money.

The sum of the monthly losses in the beginning is technically called "maximum negative cash flow." The term is not as important as the fact that you will have to include that number as part of your startup costs. In other words, you'll need money up front so that you can cover those losses and still continue to operate.

A couple on the West Coast who wanted to start a cleaning business determined their startup costs and found that their proposed business would be profitable enough to give them the income they wanted, but they would lose money the first four months, before starting to make money.

The analysis meant they would need $8000 in cash to tide them over before they could support themselves with earnings from the business. Knowing this amount ahead of time caused them to wait until they had sufficient funds, thereby avoiding what might have been serious financial problems.

Most startup costs are obvious, but accounting for negative cash flow is less obvious. Make sure you do not overlook it.

Under normal circumstances, you need to consider the purchase of certain assets, such as equipment, fixtures and inventory; buildout costs; rental deposits; construction costs; up-front advertising and marketing materials; licenses; deposits; accounting and legal fees; training, and other items. It is extremely important not to overlook any startup costs, especially if you are cutting it close. The following list might not include every startup cost you'll face, but it is a helpful reminder:

Lease deposits
Initial phone costs
Buildout costs (facility)
Utility deposits
Furniture and fixtures
Computer
Software
Training
Copies/fax/printer/scanner
Signs
Initial advertising
Initial promotion
Initial inventory
Fees to organizations/associations
Initial accounting/legal costs
Vehicle purchase
Fencing/paving/striping
Machinery/equipment
Office supplies
Initial franchise fees
Payments to banks
State/County fees
Credit card machine purchase
Fulfillment company costs
Initial storage fees
Home office modification
Adaptive/assistive equipment
License fees/tags
Web page design fees
Initial Internet charges

7. Have You Considered the Risks and Tried to Minimize Them?

There is no such thing as a no-risk business, but you can place a business on a continuum from low-risk to high-risk. Giving careful consideration to all the risks up-front can help you minimize them. Something as simple as buying business-interruption insurance can minimize many risks. But for some risks, the best you can do is make an educated guess.

If you purchase a retail store, for example, you can never be guaranteed that a competitor will not open up down the block. You can make your best guess, however, on whether a competitor is likely to open up, based on the size of the existing market, the availability of buildings, the investment required, growth potential for the area, and other factors.

Some of the standard factors to consider when calculating risks include trends in your area, pending legislation, and any factors that might affect your ability to get a continued supply of materials, or developments that might affect continued demand for your product or service.

Is the demand for your product or service concentrated in just a few customers? Do you have only one or two sources of supply? Are there any factors that would affect your ability to perform in this business? Is there likely to be greater pressure on your profit margins in the months ahead?

How about the competition? A woman with a tanning salon and exercise tables in the northeastern U.S. was doing well for her first year, but three competitors opened up in the second year, forcing her to sell at a loss. She had "direct competition." You should also be aware of "concept competition." A couple that had invested in a small bottled water company met unexpected competition when home water filters became popular in their area.

Are there special skills required to operate your business, and if you don't have them, can you easily hire someone with the right skills? A gas station owner who couldn't replace a skilled mechanic lost a lot of business. Is the proposed business complex, requiring careful management of many different factors? If so, be sure you can manage them, and check out whether specialized software might help make it less complex.

8. Why Are You Qualified to Run This Business?

Some businesses require a certain type of personality. Is your personality suitable to the business you want to open? Some businesses require certain experience or abilities if you are truly going to be in control. Do you have that experience or those abilities? Some businesses require an exceptional sales personality. Others pose a lot of stress. Some require long hours. Others are relatively "lonely" businesses, in that they provide little chance for social interaction.

When you consider the nature of your business, and how it would operate day in and day out, it's important to know that this type of business would be compatible with your personality, values, and priorities.

If you're purchasing a business, carefully assess your own suitability for it, and whether you have the same strengths and skills that have enabled the current owner to succeed. If you will need to hire someone else to fill that role, be realistic about how much the success of the business depends on that person, how much they will cost you, and how much control you have over whether they stay or leave.

Chapter 5

Other Things to Consider

In addition to the questions about yourself, the process and the business, it is helpful to address the following issues:

Buying vs. Startup

There are pros and cons to both buying a business and starting your own. Usually, but not always, a startup will require less capital. The business will usually be directly connected to your own talents and experience, a natural extension of your "personal power." This aspect of startups will lend confidence, focus, and determination.

Purchasing an existing business, on the other hand, will usually provide an immediate cash flow. Because the business has been in existence for some time, it often involves less risk if it is evaluated properly beforehand.

Proper evaluation of an existing business is extremely important. You need to look for potential negatives: real estate changes; rent escalation; construction; traffic patterns; changing nature of the customer base; emerging trends that might affect demand; new types of competition; stepped up activity from existing competitors; pressures on profit margins; slow receivables; the need for larger inventories; large expenses for advertising or staying near the top of search engine listings for your category; or any other cost element that has major impact on the business.

As mentioned earlier, you also need to carefully assess your own suitability for the business, and whether you have the same strengths and skills that enabled the current owner to succeed. If you don't, and you'd have to rely on someone else for those skills, be realistic about how much the success of the business depends on that person, and how much control you have over whether they stay or leave.

If you're purchasing a business, have you checked with a lawyer and accountant to make certain that both you and the seller are getting the best tax advantages? And can you negotiate a lower price in the event that sales at the company drop in the first year?

It may be preferable to buy assets instead of stock in a company, and if the owner is expected to finance a portion of the purchase price, you might be able to negotiate that the terms and balance due can vary depending upon what happens to sales.

Business Brokers

If you're interested in buying a business but can't decide what kind of business you'd like to buy, give yourself a fast and free education about businesses for sale in your area by contacting business brokers.

Type in *Business Brokers* on your search engine bar, and you're likely to see thousands of entries. You can narrow them down by adding criteria to your search, such as *Arizona Business Brokers*. It also helps to visit the sites of business broker associations.

If you enter *businesses for sale* on your search engine bar, you'll get access to businesses that are for sale by brokers and those for sale directly by owners.

If you contact a business broker, be prepared for them to inquire how much money you have to invest, and what your income goals are. If you don't know how much you'll be able to invest, make your best guess, or tell them you want a business that will deliver an income in a specific range. Brokers will also have you sign an agreement that says you will not attempt to go around them and deal with the seller directly, thereby cutting them out of the deal. That is a reasonable request.

The Multiple and Terms of Sale

Whether you deal through brokers or go directly to business owners (some of whom can be found by typing *businesses for sale* in your Internet search engine), the basic measure you can use to compare one business with another is the "multiple" at which it is selling. There are many other measures used in various industries, but this one is universal and basic.

The "multiple" is simply the asking price divided by the amount the owner takes out of the business annually, known as "the owner's annual take." The owner's annual take includes stated income, their salaries, and any expenses that went to the personal benefit of the owner.

For example, if the owner's annual take is $75,000, and the asking price is $150,000, the multiple is 2x. If the price is $225,000, the multiple is 3x. The lower the multiple, the better for the buyer. Small, low-asset businesses commonly sell at lower multiples, while larger and more attractive businesses sell at significantly higher multiples.

If two businesses are otherwise equally attractive, and one enables you to earn $100,000 annually for an investment of $100,000, that is likely preferable to one where you need to invest $200,000 to earn $100,000 annually. Obviously the value of assets needs to be taken into account, but you need to ask yourself, what is the true value of assets if they produce only a limited amount of income, compared to a business with a smaller dollar amount of assets, but which produces a larger income.

In addition to the multiple, another basic consideration is the "terms of sale." Some owners might be willing to accept a down payment and then payment of the balance over time at low interest rates, while another owner might require the full purchase price up front. This obviously has a bearing on what you can afford. The smaller the down payment, the more you can leverage your investment.

For example, consider that you have $60,000 to invest. One seller offers a business at $60,000 that will earn $40,000 a year but wants the purchase price up front. Another offers a business at $90,000 that earns $60,000 a year, but will accept $60,000 down, and will finance the balance over three years. In each case you are paying $60,000 down, and in each case the multiple is 1.5x, but one business earns 50% more annually.

When you buy a business with a down payment, calculate the cash flow you can expect and subtract the cost of payments to the owner, including principal and interest. So, in the example above, even though the business itself might generate $60,000 annual income, if payments to the owner will be $12,000 for three years, you'll have only $48,000 to live on for those first three years, not counting growth.

While these are the basic considerations, there are hundreds of other factors that might come into play when evaluating a business. A low multiple and favorable terms might not mean much if the business is on shaky ground with an uncertain future. When things are otherwise roughly equal, though, the multiple and terms are good basic measurements to tell you how good a deal you are getting.

Lastly, if you're comparing businesses using the multiple, consider whether you'll need to make any additional investment beyond the purchase price. If so, you'll need to calculate two multiples, one based on the asking price, and one based on the total amount you will need to invest in the business up front. For you, the most important multiple is the one based on your total investment.

Startups That Are Franchises

If you intend to start a business by buying a franchise, you might be interested in the example of a man who bought three franchises of a large, successful chain of sandwich shops. One location succeeded wildly, one was marginal, and one failed. Same franchise, different locations, which illustrates the principle that franchises are not guarantees of success. They provide three important basics – a proven identity, a marketing approach, and an operating system – but these alone do not guarantee success.

The business itself needs to be analyzed just as critically as any other business you might think of starting. Location, knowledge, experience, and the ability to sell, are the key factors in determining whether the franchise will be a success.

Can You Expand Your Options?

Building more positive beliefs about yourself, as discussed earlier, is one way to expand options. There are others:

Joining With or Employing Others. If you're not good at selling, join with someone who is. If you can sell but can't physically perform the functions that will deliver value, such as tree trimming, window washing, landscaping, carpentry, etc., join with someone who can.

You may be able to join an existing company as part owner. A man in mechanical contracting, mentioned earlier, joined a small firm where his talents in project management and bid proposals made him valuable even though he couldn't direct physical activities on site. The principal owner directed the physical aspects, so their skills complemented each other nicely.

The man bought a 25% ownership interest in the business with a down payment, with the balance to come out of future profits. A relatively simple legal agreement protected his compensation and share of the profits as a percentage of the principal owner's, even though he was only a minority shareholder.

A woman in Colorado started a trucking business. She was skillful in winning contracts but not in driving, repairing or maintaining trucks. As part of her plan, she identified reliable, talented individuals who could perform these functions and arranged for their future hire at agreed upon rates.

Technologies, Assistive Devices, and Therapies. If your disability prevents you from functioning effectively in a business, there are many advances that might help. For example:

- For the visually impaired, screen magnification is one option but scanner/synthesizer technology can also help. This technology reads printed or typed documents aloud, at various speeds, so all that is needed is training in listening/concentration.

- Voice recognition software helps those with carpal tunnel syndrome to operate a computer without pain.

- Mechanical adaptations, including platforms, hoists, hydraulic adjustable-height tables and other devices, help many people operate businesses they could not otherwise consider, including a man who operated a print and platemaking shop, and a woman who went into business as an independent seamstress.

- Some new drugs enable people to feel less pain without the drowsiness experienced from older drugs.

- Movement therapies, such as *Feldenkrais* and *Alexander Technique,* increase people's mobility to the point where they can effectively operate a business.

Training / Retraining. If you have a natural interest in a field, training will give you the skills you need to get started. One man started a successful taxidermy business after taking training from one of the leading practitioners in the field.

You've Got To Do It Yourself

Most people contemplating a business understand the DIY mentality, but a small percentage are under the mistaken impression that they can decide amongst the options after someone else has explored their business opportunities and presented the choices. That just doesn't work.

The only way you can build enough confidence and enthusiasm to make a business successful is to get out there yourself and talk with prospective customers, other people in the business, suppliers, and any others whose input and feedback might affect your business. There is simply no substitute for firsthand personal experience in this process.

Working in the Business Is a Good Idea

Years ago a client was sure he was ideally suited for a packaging and mailing business. Knowing his temperament, I suspected otherwise, and asked him to contact a similar business in some other part of the state, inquiring if he could work for them for a week at no pay. He did as I suggested, but it didn't require a week. A few days were more than sufficient to tell him he didn't want any part of that business.

Experiencing a business firsthand is especially important if you are buying an existing business. Only by being active in it on a daily basis can you tell if the business is what you think it is, and whether you are truly suited for it. Many people who think they want to buy a liquor store, bar, or convenience store, find out otherwise after they work in the business for a few weeks. Others have found it is precisely what they want.

Conclusion

If you're thinking of buying or starting a business, there's probably a good reason for it, and a lot of reasons why you are well suited to that particular business. The fastest and most direct way to make it a reality is to get started as soon as possible with an action-oriented plan, which will very quickly bring you up against the reality of that business. You will either become more confident, or realize it wasn't such a good idea.

Create a plan, even if it is only a very simple one, and be sure to get personally and intensely involved in the planning. Be sure to address all of the eight basic questions about the business. Be absolutely certain you have good answers for that all-important Question #4 about how you'll get enough sales.

Whether you create the plan yourself or get professional assistance (it's something I do for my clients, paid for by the insurance company), just be sure you've got good answers to all those questions. Ideally, you'll put together a three-year, month-by-month financial projection for how you expect the business to grow and perform financially. Even if you're only guessing, the process will sharpen your focus and cause you to ask yourself tough questions about how you'll build sales day-by-day.

Be prepared for the emotional rollercoaster. If it doesn't happen, great. But if it does, you'll be better prepared to push through the initial bouts of fear and doubt. Don't be afraid to drop a business idea if it doesn't look promising. It's part of your progress toward your eventual goal, one far more suitable for you.

Don't hesitate to drop the idea of a business altogether if your efforts tell you that you're not cut out for it. Only a small percentage of people are. Be guided by your feelings, which are the result of thoughts and questions we may not be consciously aware of, but which are significant. Bad feelings indicate that at a subconscious level, you've already figured out something's not such a good idea.

Be creative in addressing roadblocks. Perhaps you could join with someone else, or get financing from a source other than your first choice. Perhaps the location you want is not the only good location for the business.

Sometimes assistive devices make feasible a business that would otherwise be impossible for someone with a disability. A client who started a mobile mill business cutting up logs, and another who started a welding business, both relied on hydraulics, forklifts and hoists to operate.

Lastly, whenever possible, get personally involved in operating the business before making a commitment, and make sure that you are right for it. A business might be fine for someone else, but wrong for you, or vice versa. The only way to know is through firsthand experience.

Once you decide a business is for you, if you go ahead, abandon all doubt. Keep a vision of nothing but success and abundance in your head. Give it as much time and energy as your physical condition will properly allow, and plow ahead with action.

It can also be helpful to adopt the "magical approach." Using this approach, you assume that things will surely work out for the positive, and that all problems will be easily overcome. In doing so, you will minimize negative energies, fears, and anxieties.

When you spend too much time thinking about all the things that could go wrong, it tends to diminish your confidence and energy. When, on the other hand, you approach daily challenges with the assumption that you will be able to find a smooth way past them, you will, more often than not. Think of it as creating a "positive force field" that attracts success to you!

An old but good book to read in that regard, recommended to me by two clients, is *Excuse Me, Your Life is Waiting,* by Lynn Grabhorn.

Chapter 6

Learning From Examples

Here are some stories about people who started or purchased businesses, and what they learned while researching information for the business plan. These examples might give you ideas on what you need to learn for your business. In each case, the person either learned something that reaffirmed a particular market was a good one, or they made changes to help make the business more profitable.

Each of these clients got started off on the right foot, with a sound plan, enough capital to last them until projected breakeven, and an analysis that indicated they had a reasonable chance to succeed.

Every business has risk, however, and there are no statistics on how they progressed over the long term. As part of any plan, we attempt to identify all potential risks so the client enters the business fully aware of the potential pitfalls, and does whatever is possible at the outset to minimize them.

Curves Franchise in Pennsylvania

A client researching this popular workout franchise for women learned a lot from the company. He needed to research the experience of other franchisees for our business plan, though. By doing so, he determined that, at the prices he intended to charge, he needed 400 customers to net $4400 a month after lease costs and labor and franchise fees, but before other expenses.

He also had a fairly accurate notion of how long it would take him to reach that level. He also had an awareness of how many months he'd need to operate at a loss before the business turned a profit. That information was essential in order to estimate the amount he needed for startup capital.

He also became aware of an unexpected issue: whether women

prospects would relate as well to a male owner as they did to female owners of the franchises. Given his background in sales, he decided he'd have no problem there, but he was pleased to at least be aware of the issue, and made sure he had some female employees in key positions.

Taxidermy and Outfitting in Kentucky

A man in Kentucky intended to operate a taxidermy and outfitting business, and knew he'd do well with deer heads and turkeys. While researching statistics, he was surprised to learn that 18,000 non-resident fishing licenses sold in the area each year, and that he would probably do equally well with fish and ducks.

He was also pleased to learn that, for the outfitting business where he planned to guide hunters two months a year, advertising on a particular website doubled the sales for a friend of his already in the business.

That friend had far more bookings than he could accommodate, and was operating at 5 times my client's estimates for his business. The friend booked people from all over the country and even offered to send my client his overflow customers. That was reassuring to know when putting in estimated outfitting revenues for the plan.

Convenience Store in New Hampshire

A client in New Hampshire was planning to purchase a convenience store. The location was good, since the town was large enough to support profitable revenues, but not so large that it would attract chain store competition. The client, however, wanted to improve both revenues and profitability.

While gathering information for the plan and making calculations, he realized that the gross profit margin on deli items was 62%, compared to 11% for gas and 34% for grocery items. This information helped him plan for a mix of products that was more heavily weighted to deli items. He changed the store layout to do it. The plan worked well and he substantially increased profits over the previous owner in the first year.

Home Builder in the Pacific Northwest

A home builder who previously built homes costing a million dollars or more had decided to re-enter the market by building homes in the $150,000 to $200,000 range, where there was strong demand. His research with real estate agents, other builders, city officials and others, however, uncovered that large contractors with low cost structures were active in that segment, and that a small contractor would not be able to compete.

His research further uncovered that there would likely be strong demand for several years in the $200,000 to $325,000 range, where large builders would not be attracted, and where the number of houses he could build in a year was only a small fraction of anticipated demand. He chose to enter that segment, knowing it offered strong demand with suitable profit margins and less competition.

Home Repair in Nebraska

In Nebraska, a client and his wife planned to start a home repair and maintenance business, but they weren't sure of demand for their services. During their research, they learned there were 65,000 homes in their targeted zip codes, with only six firms serving them.

They further learned that many of these homes were owned by couples where both worked and didn't have time to do repairs themselves, or by retired people who couldn't do repairs themselves.

They also learned they could easily network in their local church, using a large percentage of the parishioners to spread the word for them. In addition, they knew people with lots of contacts in local associations and clubs, further increasing their network.

This same couple learned of a man who had recently retired from the business, who told them he always had as much work as he wanted, and who worked most of the time. As a result of their research, they could proceed knowing that they had a very good chance of attracting as many customers as our plan called for, very likely producing an income greater than their targeted income.

An Arts / Crafts / Gift Store in Indiana

A woman who knew several artists and sculptors decided to open a store selling their work plus less expensive gifts in Indiana, near the Ohio River, in a location frequented by tourist and recreation traffic. She hadn't done any research that indicated such a store would be successful, but agreed to get started on it.

Her research included an analysis of foot traffic in the area, and observation of the average dollar purchase in a similar store, which was $30, with roughly three items sold in the $15 category to every two sold in the $30 category and one in the $80 and up category. She also learned that traffic was extremely heavy on Saturday, and that January through April were slow months.

This information helped her decide when to open the store, and it guided her selection of the merchandise mix to offer. It also confirmed that, with the existing foot traffic, she stood an excellent chance of reaching her financial goals for the business.

A Bucket Loader Business in New England

A woman in New England planned to start a business using her bucket loader to grade driveways and lawns, to move mulch and piles of snow, and to clean stables. She also considered purchasing an augur bit to drill holes for fence posts and light installations. Research showed, however, that given the prices she had to charge, there simply wasn't enough of a market to make the business worthwhile.

She learned that if she were able to purchase a backhoe and a snow plow attachment, she could get additional work digging trenches, removing stumps, landscaping, moving rocks, and plowing snow. These additional revenue streams might make the business worthwhile.

The information guided her to plan to add a backhoe and snow plow attachment during her first year, and to actively go after those additional markets with a flyer, word of mouth and advertising.

A Dog Grooming / Treat Baking / Retailing Business in Iowa

A young woman in Iowa wanted to open a dog grooming business on the main street of a farming town in Iowa. She also liked to bake dog treats and wanted to incorporate that business at the same time. She wasn't sure, but she thought it might be a good idea to sell dog food and toys as well.

She spent a month researching all three businesses, and learned some interesting things. She found out there was very little competition in dog grooming, and that a man who had started a similar business in a similar town 50 miles away had become successful in two years, increasing the business tenfold.

She also learned that there was strong demand for a dog food retailer right in town, and that she could sell it at a good profit margin. For the dog treat business, however, research told her that while she might sell a lot of it with minimal advertising, the time required and the other expenses would make it only marginally profitable.

As a result, she understood that she needed to put her time and effort into the more profitable segments of the proposed business. She changed her plan and opened the dog grooming business in the downtown location where she also sold the dog food and toys, while she put the dog treat business on hold.

She called when she was a year into the business, to let me know she was right on plan and couldn't be happier doing what she loved. I was particularly pleased with her success, because she used the jingle I created for her radio advertising.

An Apparel Screen Printing Business in New Hampshire

A client in New Hampshire planned to start an apparel screen printing business, printing logos, designs and names on shirts, hats, sweatshirts and jackets. He was intending to serve mainly retail customers, teams, social/civic groups, and individuals within a 15-mile radius of his town.

After researching the markets, however, he totally changed his business concept. He still planned to service the retail sector, but expanded it to include trades professionals, schools, camps and clubs, restaurants, sponsored road races and other markets he had learned about.

More importantly, he learned that he could immediately service a substantial wholesale market by selling to three retail shops in the area and to one person who sold advertising specialties where company logos had to be imprinted. This market was immediate and much larger than retail. While not as profitable, its gross margins were large enough to be attractive to him.

Best of all, one of the shop owners formerly in the screen printing business found the retail end more profitable, so she had contracted out the printing and stored all her equipment. She offered to sell it to my client at a fraction of its cost if he agreed to do the printing for her. He was happy to do that since it reduced his initial investment and gave him a guaranteed large customer.

His final business model included serving a large wholesale market immediately, which generated enough income to support a good retail location. This also gave him the time he needed to build up the retail business while still reaching desired income levels.

A Pipe Carving Business in Illinois

When I first spoke with this client, he knew there was a market for the type of pipes he sold -- large freehand pipes with intricate carvings and a "one-of-a-kind sculpture" feeling. He just didn't know how large the market was, and he wasn't precisely sure how he'd go about generating sales.

He was eager to research it, though, and found that he could easily command a price of $300 per pipe for the quality of work he did, and he could probably charge twice that in two years as his reputation grew. Even more encouraging was the information he uncovered about the market and how it could be reached. He learned the market was larger than he thought, and consisted mainly of collectors in the U.S. and Europe who might or might not smoke the pipes. Each of these collectors could potentially buy a large number of pipes, not just two or three.

He also confirmed his initial impression that many carvers sold their pipes at shows like the one in Chicago he attended. He also learned something he hadn't suspected -- that many carvers sold 30 to 40 pipes at a major show, and that some would sell out their entire stock (75 or more) at prices higher than he intended to charge. Further, he confirmed that only one other man offered the type of pipes he would offer. That other man had only a few of them for sale. My client's pipes were of equal or better quality when compared to the competition.

Most important for purposes of his business, he learned he could lecture and display at regional meetings of collectors, at no cost. He hadn't been aware of these meetings, which were held quite frequently. Sales potential at these meetings was significant and provided him a platform to build his reputation.

He was pleased to learn about the role of the internet in the business, and the power of advertising and publicity in newsletters and a major trade magazine.

As a result of his research, we were able to put together a cost effective sales and marketing strategy for him. He could proceed with the business knowing that within two years, he could build a reputation and generate sales for almost as many pipes as he could make. This would meet his modest income goals for the business, allowing him to generate most of the income he needed by doing something he loved.

Small and Medium Engine Repair in Oklahoma

A client in Oklahoma wanted to start a mobile engine repair business, serving mainly farm trucks and tractors on-site within a one-hour drive from his home, but he had no idea how large his market was. During his research, he expanded his target market to include boats, oil pumps and riding lawn mowers. He determined that, for the small and medium engine markets, there were an estimated 150,000 units in his service area, and only two other shops provided mobile service. Both were turning away business because they were 2 to 4 weeks behind.

In addition to discovering that his market was much larger than he realized, he learned of relatively inexpensive ways to attract customers. Then he learned that the markup on parts was larger than he had anticipated.

He decided to work from a small building he would construct on his own property, to keep costs low. The new knowledge enabled us to develop financial projections with solid, conservative projections, assuming only gradual growth, that showed income of about $40,000 in the first year, but which climbed close to the $100,000 range for the 2nd and 3rd years.

Scaling Back a Proposed Mechanical Repair / Storage / Office Rental Business in North Dakota

This client and his business partner proposed to start a mechanical repair and maintenance business in two locations, serving buses, delivery trucks and fertilizer spreaders in the surrounding farming areas. Their plan called for either leasing or purchasing a building with far more space than they needed, and using that space to generate income via storage and office rentals.

During the research phase, my client learned that they would not be able to negotiate the favorable terms on the building they had hoped for, and so they wisely scaled back the proposed business, focusing only on the repair and maintenance functions in existing low-overhead properties.

They also learned they might not get as much of the service business as originally assumed, so we developed primary financial projections using scaled-back assumptions. As is customary, we developed alternate projections showing what would happen if revenues were lower than primary projections, in this case 70% of the primary.

As a result of the research and scaled back operations, my client found he could get by during the first year even at the 70% projections, while in the 2nd and 3rd years income would meet his goals.

As a result of developing this plan, he had avoided what might have been a costly mistake, and could now look forward to income from scaled back operations that would meet his goals without taking undue risk. He also avoided having to make any substantial startup expenditures and did not need to commit himself to future financial obligations that might have been difficult to meet.

Defining How to Structure an Executive Protection Service

A client in the Washington, D.C. area formerly worked for the FBI. Among his many assignments was a key position of responsibility for the protection of three different Attorneys General of the United States. He was eminently qualified to operate an executive protection business, but wasn't yet clear on what specific services to offer and how to operate the business.

As a result of meeting with many people in and around the industry, he determined that it would be best to offer three distinct services – threat assessment and risk analysis, on-site training in protective operations procedures, and temporary protective services for individuals who needed to supplement their existing protection.

Given his contacts and experience, we planned a gradual buildup of his business using only networking and selected distribution of a brochure we developed, with letters targeted to specific individuals, referencing third parties known to the recipient in the opening of the letters.

As a result of all his hard work researching the market and the services most in demand, he gained a firm understanding of not only the best ways to build the business, but also, in practical everyday terms, how he would operate it.

Our projections showed that, assuming only modest growth in the first three years, he could reach a net income exceeding

$100,000, which fit well with his overall financial needs and planning. Since he also felt a strong need to remain active and productive, he could proceed with confidence to build a business that would keep him fulfilled in that regard.

A Specialty Retailer in Northwest Texas

A relatively isolated town in Texas with a population of only 25,000 -- and only 50,000 in the trading area -- might not seem like the ideal location to open a retail shop. As often as not, factors like that rightly discourage people intent on opening a retail store because of the associated risks.

Every case is unique, however, and a client in his mid 30's had done his homework. He and his wife had experience selling eyeglasses and scented candles, and he'd had discussions with people he knew in town as well as his teenage son, nephew and friends. He concluded there was strong demand in the area for a mix of about a dozen types of products.

He was confident that if he sold just a few specific products, and kept his overhead low, he could sell enough even in a poor economy to meet his income goals and be active in a productive, enjoyable life.

Following normal procedure, I instructed him to do extensive research on costs, pricing and quality for each proposed line, and on available store sites and lease terms, costs of advertising and promotion, and the best ways to build word-of-mouth awareness of the store.

Frankly, I was surprised by his intensity and creativity in researching and negotiating everything he would need. We originally estimated his rent would be at least $700 a month, but he was able to secure a good facility in a good location for just $300 ... with guaranteed caps on increase upon renewal. And did you know that quality polarized sunglasses, knock-offs of major brands, can be purchased for about $32.00/dozen? Some major chains sell a single similar pair for $19.00!

After a month of whirlwind activity, we had detailed figures on prices for high quality t-shirts, jerseys, sunglasses, skateboards, pocket knives, handbags, jewelry, candles, caps, belts, and miscellaneous low-priced toys, novelties and other items for young children. We also knew what they sold for at towns 60 miles away. This client figured to ensure his success by offering high quality items at much lower prices.

He obtained detailed information on costs for all radio and print advertising and promotional activities, signs, and other items that were part of his marketing plan. He even had slogans and jingles prepared. In the course of his research, he also changed some of his assumptions, refined his product mix and message, and solidified his pricing structure for each item based on costs and competitive information.

Our highly detailed plan with three sets of projections showed that, using conservative assumptions on revenues, he could expect to generate about $35,000 of income the 1st year, growing to $45,000 in the 3rd year. These projections fit well with his financial plans.

Thanks to free help from relatives and friends, his startup costs were relatively modest. Between the insurer and the State of Texas, he was able to get the money he needed to start this business. Because he planned so carefully and realistically based on firsthand feedback from potential customers, he significantly lowered the risk level for a startup retail business that is designed to do well even in difficult economic times.

Child Care in New England

Here is a business in a category that often succeeds... a service business... with established demand on a broad basis... and easily identified potential customers.

Child care fits that definition. A New England woman in her late 30's with experience in the field wanted to start a business using only her home on a small scale, then expanding to a larger at-home

65

business, then eventually to a much larger business from a leased facility where teen counseling would be added.

In a sense, this plan was so surely going to be a success, you could almost say she did not need a plan; however, she was very grateful to the insurer for having us develop one. At the conclusion of our involvement, she mentioned some of the benefits:

She could meet her income goals in the first two years with just the smallest scale and working only four days per week. This schedule would leave time for her to complete studies toward a degree required for teen counseling and to care for her four children.

She now knew exactly what she needed to spend to get started in the business.

She learned her market and her pricing were not what she thought they would be before she did the research for the plan, so her actions were now more realistic.

She learned she'd be better off staying small and not hiring helpers as she had planned, because the additional income was not worth the extra time and effort.

She had more peace of mind as she proceeded, with a clear vision of how she wanted to operate the business.

Interesting Side Story: Her disability was chronic neck and back pain due to a motor vehicle accident, but she told me that several years earlier she had been suffering for years from what doctors diagnosed as fibromyalgia. She learned of a clinic in New Mexico and spoke with the woman who runs it, who told her it was not fibromyalgia, but a virus. She was treated there for two weeks and has not had any symptoms since. It is just an anecdote, of course, but interesting.

Expanding a Music Creation Business in New Jersey

A client in New Jersey had a six-year-old partnership that created, composed, arranged and recorded music, but revenues had ranged only from $4000 to $10,000. I was asked to develop a plan for an expanded operation that would generate more income.

The client and his business partner were both very enthusiastic, took the initiative to do all the recommended research, and brainstormed with me on the best new ways to build revenues. At the end they were quite appreciative, because they now had:

- A sound plan that showed various scenarios they considered realistic, indicating income for each partner that ranged from $80,000 to $120,000, depending on how quickly and to what extent they could build revenues.

- Clear priorities as to how much time and effort would be devoted to each of seven market segments we had identified, and well-defined action steps for building revenues in the top segments.

- An accurate understanding of monthly expenses.

- Confidence from knowing they needed only $11,000 to expand as aggressively as possible. With the written plan, they could probably attract that much capital and more from friends, relatives and business associates.

Awakening the Inner Author for a Consulting Business

A client in the State of Washington had been a management consultant for non-profits and small for-profit businesses. His disability limited his energy and mobility somewhat, but he could work up to 7 hours a day, drive for an hour, and lift 25 pounds. An independent consultancy was ideal for him, but he needed to build revenues and income.

Once I understood his past achievements and background, and the markets he was best positioned to serve, I recommended that:

- He write a self-published e-book based on his past writings, to be available in print as well, that would give him credibility with prospects and also be useful in delivering his services.

- We develop a brochure that explained the benefits of using him, as well as his concept and competitive "selling propositions."

- He update his website along the lines of the brochure, complete with success stories and testimonials.

- I supply him with contact information on hundreds of his best prospects and create prototype letters for him that he could adapt when sending them the brochure; these letters would set the stage for his follow-up phone call.

- I create a "summary of credentials," a one-page document to show or send to prospects to increase credibility. A short form of the summary would be included in the brochure and the book.

He was so energized that the first thing he did was write and e-publish the book. He felt so good about this, and his confidence increased so much as he began to appreciate his own talents and value more, that it unleashed a torrent of energy. I wrote the letters, drafted the brochure, supplied the contacts, taught him how to find more contacts, and critiqued his website upgrade.

He wound up writing his own business plan, which was quite good, and he developed a lot of new business prospects in the short time span of my involvement (about two months).

I had given myself credit for helping him in several ways, but he brought me back to earth by telling me that the most valuable thing to him was simply my sharing a process for selling consulting services. Something clicked as soon as he understood this, he said, and he could immediately envision how to approach prospects in a very powerful way, increasing his energy and confidence.

A Barge Boat in Louisiana

Most of us seldom think about the barge industry. That's fine with the people in it. They don't care about publicity and glamour, content instead with outsized profits. Transportation by barge is a huge industry. It is much cheaper than rail, and just about any commodity you can think of is shipped this way – stones, grain, corn, salt, fertilizer, coal, etc.

The nature of the industry presents an opportunity for any business that owns the boats that push the barges. I had no idea that a 65-foot boat could push six 195-ft. by 35-ft. barges, aligned in two rows of three. The area pushed amounts to approximately 600 ft. long by 70 ft. wide. And that's just a small boat!

Most of the time, every available boat is busy. It's been a stable business for a long time, essential to the movement of basic commodities for which there is constant global demand. If you're like me, you probably didn't realize that boats pushing barges from Louisiana routinely travel to northern and northeastern cities. There are risks, of course, but fewer than in most industries.

So why isn't everyone in the barge business? Because there's a catch. You not only need enough money to buy or lease a boat, but a good enough reputation so that the shippers will give you regular business. You need a reliable boat in very good condition, or must know how to find one at a good price for either purchase or lease, and you've got to know a lot about operations and hiring reliable crews.

My client, in his 50s, scored well on all three counts. He had worked his way up from deck hand to Captain before his disability sidelined him. Theoretically he could go into business as an owner who hired others to do all the physical work, but he didn't have the money to buy or lease a boat.

Enter the business plan. It showed that the business could realistically earn a substantial amount of money each month, right from the start! Long story short, the insurer was happy to settle with him for an amount that let him cover his first month's boat lease payment and all other startup expenses. He was thrilled to get back into action and secure his financial future at the same time.

By Now, You Get the Idea

All of these examples were very distinct types of businesses, with few similarities to one another. But there are certain constants you need to look for in starting or buying any business.

By far, the most important factors are having some idea of the nature and size of your market, and knowing with confidence that you have a reasonable chance of generating the kind of sales volume you need to generate profits.

One of the best ways to do that, if you can, is to "triangulate" your research findings by using three different bases for your estimates: feedback from prospective clients, industry information, and confirmation from fellow business owners.

For example, if you talk to a lot of prospective customers and they indicate they will buy from you at a certain level, that's one basis for projecting sales.

If you then get information from an industry association about average sales for the type of business you want to start, and it reinforces what you learned from the prospects, that gives you a stronger basis for making assumptions about sales forecasts.

If you then contact people in the business in other parts of the country, and their input confirms what you learned from prospects and industry figures, you now have information from three separate sources that tracks roughly along the same lines. You can then make your sales estimates with greater confidence.

Chapter 7

What Action Steps Can You Take Now?

If you are reading this book, that's step #1. It gives you a framework for deciding whether you really want to start a business, and if so, it provides guidelines for identifying a business you can get excited about.

If you find a business you can get excited about, then step #2 is to get a rough estimate of likely startup costs. If they are going to be substantial and you don't have the money, you can ask the insurance company that holds your long term disability policy if they can help you.

Your insurance company might be helpful in one of three ways:

Offsets

Insurance companies can continue to pay your benefit while asking you to send them earnings reports on a monthly, quarterly or other basis. If your reports show net income in a given period, they can then offset the benefit payment by the amount of the earnings.

So if you earn $1000 in a given month, for example, they could deduct $1000 from your next payment. A company will usually continue this type of support until your net income reaches a certain percentage of pre-disability earnings – often, but not always, 80%.

Vocational Rehabilitation Budgets

The person working with you in Vocational Rehabilitation might or might not have a small budget, usually less than $5000, to help with expenditures like a computer and software, a printer/copier/fax, and other items commonly required for operating a business.

In some instances they can approve specialized training or education that would give you the credentials required to win a job in a particular field. Budgets here vary widely from one insurer to another.

Settlements

Some people ask the insurer to "settle" their policies in order to get the capital required. "Settling" usually means that they receive a sum of money from the insurance company, and in return they give up any claims they may have to benefits under the policy. The settlement may be structured in such a way that the insured doesn't get all cash, but a combination of cash and an annuity, for example, to provide an element of security.

In the event that a settlement might be of interest to you, here are a few thoughts that might prove helpful. This is an area where there is a lot of misunderstanding, and there tends to be an element of mystery about it.

Some insurers will not consider settlements. Among those that will, they might be open to settlement at one point in time, but have no interest at another time. Insurers are not obliged to settle a claim. They may choose to continue paying your monthly benefit.

While insurers are not obliged to settle a long term disability claim, they may do so if it can be shown that it would be beneficial to the claimant and to themselves. When insurers are happy to settle, it is usually because they can be reasonably assured it will be financially beneficial to a person who has a sound business plan, and because they will free up reserves and get some liabilities off their books.

For example, if they are paying you $3000 per month until age 65 and you are 45, then theoretically they could be paying you $36,000 for 20 years, or a total of $720,000. A lot of people mistakenly think that if they settle, that's the amount they should get.

Insurers don't see it that way. The people who determine what you'll be offered are not those in Vocational Rehabilitation, but rather, people on the financial side who think about the "present value of money." They use various calculations that result in putting money into reserves for paying that claim. You might think the amount of money would be the amount needed for safe investments to generate enough money to pay your claim each month, but it's not that simple.

Using complex calculations, they figure out formulas and multipliers for certain categories. If your case falls into one of these categories, there isn't much you can do about it. The amount of the offer will be smaller, for example, if you fall into a category where most people go back to work in a few years, or if you are likely to recover from your disability. Depending on the nature of your disability and the terms of your policy, there may be varying degrees of probability as to whether you will still qualify for benefits after certain periods.

Although it's not a clearcut area, if you request a settlement and it makes sense from the insurer's standpoint (often it doesn't), they are likely to come back with an offer. It is, however, difficult to know what an insurer will offer you. Don't be shocked if the offer is 30% or less of what you'd get if you received benefit payments over the full term of the policy. The offer also may not be open to negotiation. Sometimes it is negotiable, but many times it is not.

Consider all your options carefully. Some people don't think the settlement offer is large enough and they get annoyed, withdrawing their settlement request. Others calculate that the offer, while not as large as they had wanted, is still large enough to start or buy a business that will generate the level of earnings they want, so they settle. I do not make recommendations here. It is up to each individual, based on his or her unique circumstances.

It is often wise to consult a lawyer. Some insurers strongly recommend that you do. Just be sure to retain one who is familiar with long term disability settlements. Long term disability settlements are NOT the same as settlements of Workers Compensation claims.

In one case, I worked for months with a fellow to get a food wholesaling business off the ground, with the clear understanding that any settlement would likely be within a certain range. Everything looked positive until, at the last moment, his lawyer demanded 10 times what the insurer was offering. The insurer withdrew the offer.

Other financing possibilities

In years past, when states had more money to spend, it was possible to get some financial support from your State's Department of Economic Development, particularly the small business department. Likewise, in good economic times, banks could serve as another source. If you brought your plan to two banks and got turned down, you could approach the Small Business Administration for a loan guarantee.

In difficult times, possibilities are more limited. With a sound business plan, though, if the insurance company can't help, you might consider presenting your case to small investor groups in your area, so-called "angel investors," or you might approach wealthy individuals, offering them attractive interest rates on their investment (if your proposed business is capable of paying them).

You can also approach successful people established in the kind of business you want to operate, but you need to be wary of their bypassing you and starting the business without your involvement. Lastly, you might gain favorable consideration from friends and relatives by offering attractive interest rates on their investment. If you can interest several of them, the individual risk each one takes might be small enough that they are willing to invest.

The Element of Risk

If your proposed business is risky and you need your benefit payments to live on, it's probably not a good idea to ask for a settlement. You may find that the insurer is unwilling to consider one if you do ask, especially if you don't have a sound plan or any entrepreneurial experience. The same holds true if there's a good chance that, for health reasons, you will have to cut back your business involvement before you get the business to a point that someone else can take over.

Some people with substantial resources do not need their benefit payments to live on. They are quite happy to take their chances, even in a risky business. But if you depend even partially on benefits to meet your living expenses, remember that if your business fails, you are left with no income from the business and no benefit payments. And if the business is not generating income, it's not likely to be worth very much if you attempt to sell it.

Step #3

Action step #3 is to define your business as accurately as you can, and then research your market and the specific steps you will take to build revenues. If the business continues to look promising, get back to your insurance company and ask if they can provide someone to help you develop a business plan.

They might provide someone like me, or in some cases they might refer you to SCORE, or to a local business college. These resources can be very helpful, but the quality and depth of assistance will vary substantially based on the individuals involved and the amount of time they can devote to you. It certainly doesn't hurt to inquire and find out what they can do for you.

Regardless, if you feel highly positive about a business and you're determined to see it through, keep on going until you either start it or decide against it. Don't be easily discouraged. Instead, rely on what you find out firsthand as you explore and research, and make your own decision accordingly. Good luck!

Daniel T. McAneny

Since 1986, for over a dozen major insurers, Dan has worked one-on-one with over 2000 people on disability. He has helped people at all income levels, in a variety of previous occupations, in all parts of the U.S.

Dan started out primarily helping people find new jobs, but transitioned into mainly assisting those who want to start or buy a business, or purchase a franchise.

Dan has a broad background in business. It includes manufacturing, banking, advertising, personal marketing for job search, and consulting on business growth options. As a result, he can be effective with almost anyone, from any background. He has scrutinized thousands of careers in depth, gaining insights into many occupations and businesses.

He studied Accounting, Banking and Finance at NYU Graduate School of Business Administration, and his undergraduate degree in Sociology was earned from Holy Cross College in Worcester MA.

28978678R00044

Made in the USA
San Bernardino, CA
12 January 2016